The Story of the CAR

Peter Roberts

TREASURE PRESS

The author and publishers would like to offer their sincere thanks to the following persons and organizations for their valuable help in compiling this book, both in the matter of editorial research and illustrations: Adam Opel AG; Alfa Romeo SpA; American Motors Corporation; Automobiles Citroën; Automobiles Peugeot SA; Mr. Michael Banfield; Mr. Cecil Bendall; British Leyland UK Limited; Chrysler Corporation; Daimler-Benz AG; Fiat SpA; Ford Motor Company Limited; General Motors Corporation; Lips Autotron, Holland; Mercedes-Benz (UK) Limited; Musée de l'Automobile Française; Norddeutsches Auto Motorrad Museum; Régie Renault; Mr. Peter Richley; Rolls-Royce Motors Limited; Sotheby's; Stratford-upon-Avon Motor Museum; Vauxhall Motors Limited; Victoria and Albert Museum, Bethnal Green, London.

Thanks are extended in particular to Mr. Harry Hossent for his valuable contributions to the book.

Photographic acknowledgments
Neill Bruce: pages 14 top, 20 top, 35, 44-5, 58, 69, 76-7, 78-9, 83, 86, 94, 124. Nicky Wright: pages 31, 55, 65, 66, 88-9, 90. (The photographs on pages 88-9 and 90 are also by permission of the Auburn-Cord-Duesenberg Museum, those on pages 14 (top) and 35 by permission of the Bicton Hall of Transport, Devon, that on page 31 by permission of Mr. Goldsmith, Itchenor, Sussex, that on page 65 by permission of Harrah's Automobile Collection, Reno, Nevada, and that on page 86 by permission of the Midland Motor Museum, Bridgnorth.)
All other photographs are from the Peter Roberts Collection

Front cover: Ferrari 308 GTS, 1980 (Neill Bruce)
Back cover: Auburn 12-161A Phaeton Sedan, 1932 (Nicky Wright/Auburn-Cord Duesenberg Museum)
Title spread: Duesenberg SSJ, 1935 (Colour Library International)

First published by Optimum Books in 1983

This edition first published in Great Britain in 1989 by
Treasure Press
Michelin House
81 Fulham Road
London SW3 6RB

Produced by Mandarin Offset
Printed and bound in Hong Kong

Contents

No Horse for Frau Daimler

The Prince of Wales was enjoying himself immensely. Seated in the driving seat, grinning like a schoolboy, he piloted the machine at top speed, chatting to his somewhat nervous passenger, and plainly delighted with his newly-acquired skill in conducting the strange vehicle.

The venue was the Imperial Institute in London and the occasion, a small demonstration set up for the heir to the throne after 'His wish to try a motor car had been graciously expressed'. It was, thought entrepreneur Harry Lawson, a wonderful chance to further the cause of the Bill to change the law relating to the speed of mechanical road vehicles then before the House. A heaven-sent opportunity to publicize his 'Motor Show' to be held in a few months' time.

A light De Dion Bouton steam tricar of 1886.

Opened in the Spring of 1896, well before the British motor industry was more than a gleam in the eyes of a few far-sighted engineers, the Motor Show made its debut optimistically some six months before the laws of the land were eventually modified to allow motorists to use the public roads of Britain at a pace faster than a brisk walk.

Edward Albert, Prince of Wales, then a portly 55, had actually experienced his first spin when he had ridden in a Serpollet steam car in 1893 while on vacation at Bad Homburg in Germany, and now he was showing a strong interest in the technological developments of motor transportation.

The Prince rode in four different 'autocars' at the Institute, a Daimler, an Acme (from the Benz Co. at Mannheim), a Pennington, and an electric carriage. A day earlier he had been taken by the Hon. Evelyn Ellis for a short trip in a Daimler 'into the open . . . where Mr. Ellis, who is a fully experienced motorist, executed some skillful manoeuvres in stopping, starting and generally handling the vehicle.' England's sporting prince considered the form of locomotion fascinating, but opined that it would not entirely supersede the horse. However, he thought the sport of motoring would no doubt take its place in the leisure activities of society.

Not long afterwards, the man who became Britain's monarch, Edward VII, experienced another, more daring ride, when he was

The world's very first automobile – the steam-propelled three-wheeled carriage constructed by French engineer Nicolas Cugnot in 1770 – having the world's first road accident.

taken out by the Hon. John Scott Montagu (father of the present Lord Montagu). They and their two lady companions achieved a breath-taking 40 mph.

Thanks largely to the Prince's earlier interest, and to a small coterie of influential enthusiasts, the British motor industry was born. By November 1896 the Acts of Parliament that had restricted motoring to impossibly slow speeds were amended, and such motor vehicles as there were in the country were allowed to travel at speeds of up to 12 mph. Britain's motor age had commenced.

However, over the Channel in France and Germany there were, at this time, comparatively large numbers of expert and enthusiastic motorists on the roads, and in France several motor competitions and speed events had further fired the imagination of the public. One held during the previous year, 1895, had made a strong mark in automotive history, when a Panhard et Levassor car had won the long, hazardous

An artist's impression of the motor age meeting the horse era: predictable chaos.

The Benz car of 1885–86. With one cylinder and just under one horsepower, it was the world's first practical motor car.

race from Paris to Bordeaux and back, an astonishing distance of 1,178 kilometres (732 miles).

It was only ten years earlier that the story of the modern automobile began. Steam vehicles had been used as public transport some 50 years previously, but had eventually been outlawed from the roads by the strong commercial railway and horse interests of those who controlled legislative power. Then a second generation of much smaller and lighter steam carriages had been developed and were in current use in tiny numbers, but they were still too clumsy and inconvenient to attract much interest.

By 1880 practical engineering had developed methods of producing a small (compared with steam machinery) accurately-made cylinder and filling it with an accurately-fitting piston. Gear-cutting had become more sophisticated. Electrics had been developed; petroleum as fuel and as lubricant was available. The time was ripe for the appearance of something more practical than Lenoir's self-propelled cart of 1862 which was driven by town 'lighting' gas.

History records that two men came up with the winning answers – almost simultaneously. Karl Benz and Gottlieb Daimler, both

Germans, worked within a few miles of each other, but knew nothing of each other's activities. They produced the first practical cars, and are duly recognized as the 'fathers of the automobile'. There were undoubtedly others, whose labours blossomed unseen and unacclaimed, for as in all developments in science and engineering, the age seems to bring about numerous similar enterprises concurrently.

Daimler had learned much from the experience of his one-time employer Nikolaus Otto, who had revivified the inefficient atmospheric gas-engine by adding a compression stroke, creating the modern four-stroke sequence used in most petrol and diesel engines today.

Daimler made his first full-sized (half-horsepower!) four-stroke engine in 1885, fitted it into a crude boneshaker type of two-wheeler – and thus made the first motorcycle. Shortly afterwards he fitted a similar engine of just over one horsepower into a four-wheel carriage. He had ordered it for his wife, ostensibly as a birthday present, keeping his real purpose, that of transmogrifying it into a motor vehicle, under his top hat. Already, the police had raided his workshop at 13 Gartenstrasse in Bad Cannstatt, accusing him of making counterfeit banknotes; they had withdrawn with apologies but Daimler was suspicious of official reaction to the sight of a road vehicle without the familiar animal in the shafts. The public also distrusted the use of 'explosive' petrol.

The Daimler 'single-track' vehicle, built in the Cannstatt workshop in 1885.

His four-seater phaeton had its single-cylinder engine poking up awkwardly through the rear compartment. Ignition was obtained by a thin metal tube permanently inserted in the cylinder, kept at white-hot temperature by a bunsen burner-type flame. After enormous difficulties in controlling timing and combustion Daimler quietly tested his car in 1886. Later the discreet Württemberger made the first public tests of his engine in a motor boat, which he used on the River Neckar, covering the fact that he was using an 'explosion' engine that might have frightened spectators, by festooning the boat with wires, encouraging people to assume that it was driven by an electric motor which they, at least, would accept more readily, he considered.

Daimler's restless mind was, however, not content with powering a road vehicle and a river craft although, curiously, it was his motorboat that did much to reduce the prejudice that existed against the petrol engine, and this explains the emphasis on marine engines in early Daimler production.

He adapted his single-cylinder engine (and by 1889 his V-twin unit) to power street cars, firepumps, and even to propel successfully a one-man airship. His dream of universal application was coupled with his intention to increase the power of his engine – and just four years after building his first ½ hp device, something near 10 hp had been developed.

Demand for Daimler units increased, but the Cannstatt business really took off after the exhibiting of the prototype 'Stahlradwagen', the Steel-wheeler, a spiky, spoky, tubular four-wheeler which owed more to bicycle engineering than to the horsey past, and even more to the new two-cylinder engine round which it was built. When this new vehicle was seen at the 1889 Paris World Exposition, a contract was rapidly signed with the French company of Panhard et Levassor, of which more later.

Above: Gottlieb Daimler's first four-wheeled vehicle was completed in 1885. It was driven by a single-cylinder unit which stood exposed near the back seat of the converted phaeton.

Left: Daimler's 'Stahlradwagen' (Steel-wheeler) of 1889 housed a two-cylinder engine and was one of the first of his vehicles to break away from carriage-building tradition.

The first-ever long-distance drive. Karl Benz' wife and two sons made a pioneer journey of about 50 miles in 1888. They purchased their fuel from an Apotheke (chemist).

Meanwhile, back at Mannheim in 1885, Karl Benz, the other 'father' of the modern automobile, was hard at work developing his own engine. Several years earlier, in 1879, Karl and his young wife Bertha had experienced a sublime moment when they stood in their back-garden workshop listening to Karl's first tiny engine chugging its way into history on the workbench. Said Benz of that moment, after countless failures to start the machine: 'We were standing in front of the engine as if it were a great mystery that was impossible to solve. My heart was pounding. I turned the crank; the engine started to go put-put-put . . . we both listened to it for a full hour, never tiring of the single tone of its song. The two-cycle engine was performing as no magic flute in the world ever had . . . we knew the most heartfelt happiness that evening in our poor little workshop. . . .'

That evening, as the world's first practical internal combustion engine chattered out its rhythm, the New Year's Bells began to ring – and life as it was known began to change.

Benz' vehicle was completed in 1885 and patented on 29 January 1886. A three-wheeler (he had not yet mastered fourwheel steering principles, although they were known at the time) with a watercooled single-cylinder horizontal engine developing just less than one horse-

Benz' first four-wheeler, the Viktoria of 1893. A new jet-style carburettor and a lusty 3-hp unit were other improvements.

power at the then high speed of 250 revolutions per minute, the light car was based on a design completely divorced from traditional carriage thinking. Benz had constructed a motored car, not an adaptation of an existing type of vehicle. Everything was new in concept, from his own workshop-made ignition coil, spark plugs and surface carburettor to the system of belts and pulleys in the transmission. The first time the car was tested on a public road it reached the satisfying speed of 14 km/h (9 mph).

An improved model was shown at the Munich Engine Show in 1888 when Benz first advertised his car. A small sidelight of the interest shown by would-be motor-makers is the report that, owing to Benz' generous offer to allow visitors to test the vehicle at the Show, 'over 13,000 admission tickets were purchased by workmen' all presumably eager to start constructing their own horseless carriages.

The general public's reservations, however, says one contemporary document, 'had the same effect as frost on flowers that bloom too early,' and Karl Benz must have read with chagrin that 'although the petrol car caused some stir at the Munich Exposition, this employment of the petrol engine will probably be no more promising than the use of the steam engine for road travel.'

12

The first Benz sales brochure of 1888 did not attract any buyers at all. His family decided that they would try to promote interest in the Benz vehicle themselves. One fine morning in August 1888 while father Benz was still asleep, Frau Benz and her two sons Eugen, 15, and Richard, 18 months younger, set off on what was to become an historic trip. With Eugen at the steering lever they drove from Mannheim to Pforzheim, about 80 km (50 miles) away. Up gradients they used people-power, for fuel they called at an apothecary; a cobbler supplied leather replacement brake pads, and innkeepers gave them water and directed their route. Stretched chains, a blocked fuel line, and an ignition fault the boys repaired themselves.

The pioneer long-distance journey created quite a sensation, and has been recorded as a 'first' in the history books. But it still failed to stir the public into purchasing Benz cars. Karl Benz sold precious few vehicles until he had completed his new four-wheeled Viktoria (so-called to mark his victory over the seemingly insurmountable steering problems associated with the vehicle). His patent of 28 February 1893 for 'A steering mechanism for a car with steering circles set at a tangent to the wheels' was somewhat ironic, as a similar patent had been taken out by the coachbuilder to the Royal Court of Bavaria as early as 1816.

Sales brochure for 1898. This Benz phaeton was also made in hunting-car, landau and omnibus form.

However, the Viktoria was a much improved car, with a 3-hp engine, pulley gearchanges and a new jet carburettor; Benz himself much favoured his first Viktoria for his own family outings for a considerable time.

This car too was proved by a long-distance marathon. An Austrian industrialist, Theodor von Liebig, drove one from Bohemia to Mannheim and on to Rheims in France and back, a total of 938 km (583 miles). His fuel consumption was modest – but the vehicle used some 1,500 litres of cooling water. The car was soundly built, it was relatively reliable as transport, it was reasonably priced – but still few buyers turned up at the Benz workshops.

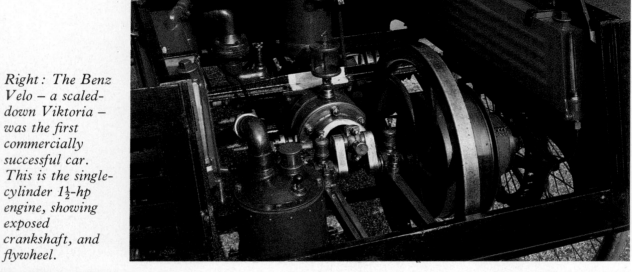

Right: The Benz Velo – a scaled-down Viktoria – was the first commercially successful car. This is the single-cylinder 1½-hp engine, showing exposed crankshaft, and flywheel.

Below: The engine was still at the back of this 1898 Benz Ideal, although fashion demanded a dummy bonnet (hood). It had a top speed of 35 km/h, 4½ horsepower and one cylinder.

Benz' master stroke was the scaling-down of the Viktoria. He called the new vehicle of 1894 the Velo. With an engine half the size of the former car, the price slashed dramatically to 2,000 marks, and the car itself more easily controlled, the Velo caught the public's imagination, and the small light two-seater began to attract buyers.

In 1895 Benz made 134 vehicles of which 62 were Velos. Others included 36 Viktorias and sundry other types including the first motor bus. Soon the Velo was being turned out in larger numbers with identical specifications – the first 'mass-produced' car. Benz also introduced the world's first motor bus service that year, with two modified eight-seater Landaus.

France was showing an interest in the German car by this time. Previously a pioneer in the self-propelled road vehicle field, that country had lost its tenuous lead to Germany with the advent of Daimler and Benz, although the tradition of the French-built steam vehicle had been kept alive by companies like Bollée, De Dion Bouton, Serpollet and others.

Importer Emile Roger of 52 Rue des Dames in Paris bought a Benz *Pferdloserwagen* (horse-free car) in 1887. He had earlier bought Benz engines for stationary work, and was eventually given a licence by Benz to assemble (later to build) and sell Benz cars in France as his sole agent. Engineer Roger is credited with a significant hand in the design and building of the four-wheeled Viktoria – and through his enthusiastic efforts, with sparking off the first French interest in automobilism.

Schoolfriends Emile Levassor and René Panhard had graduated at the Ecole Centrale, Paris, gone their separate ways in engineering, later joining up again to form the company of Panhard et Levassor.

At the Paris Exposition of 1889, Levassor saw the new Daimler car, sniffed at its construction – but thought the engine was worth investigating. Now some years earlier Daimler had assigned a licence to attorney Edouard Sarazin, an old friend of Levassor, to build his

Three of Benz' daughters pose for a picture in one of their father's horseless carriages in 1894.

engines (one should remember that his engines were in use for some time before he made his first car) and granted him exclusive rights to produce them in France. Sarazin died suddenly in 1887 and his widow, the attractive Louise Sarazin, inherited the contract.

Emile Levassor had built one or two engines for testing purposes, and accompanied Mme. Sarazin to Stuttgart to confer with Gottlieb Daimler. A romance ensued. In 1889 she was officially given exclusive rights as distributor of Daimler engines in France. In 1890 Levassor married the lady, and under French law became the owner of those rights.

Both Daimler and Levassor met an important French cycle-manufacturing family, the Peugeots, at Valentigney. They had made their fortune producing metal stays for the crinoline dresses of an earlier period, but when the fashion faded they had turned them into bicycle spokes. Armand, one of the sons, had also started experimenting with steam cars. He soon abandoned the Serpollet steam engine when he saw the Daimler product, by then a V-twin unit. By 1891 he had built his first Panhard-Daimler engined quadricycle.

He was beaten by a whisker by the astute Levassor, who produced his first car on 17 February 1890, a vehicle which had its first public run early the next year, from the works at Avenue d'Ivry in Paris to the Pont-du-Jour about 10 km (6 miles) away – with continual breakdowns. This first car had its engine placed midships, right under the passenger seats. An old picture shows an uncomfortable Mme. Levassor in the hot seat, and that may even be one of the reasons for the rapid change of layout to a front-engined plan – although it is more likely that weight distribution and steering problems were the prime

One of the first Peugeot motor vehicles, the 1892 Vis-à-Vis, with rear-mounted Daimler V-twin engine.

causes. History does acknowledge, however, that the Panhard of 1891 was the first to provide subsequent designers with what was to become the traditional layout of cars – engine at the front followed by flywheel, clutch, a gearbox giving a choice of indirect ratios, and bevel drive to a cross shaft and side chains to the rear wheels – the *Système Panhard*. Six cars were made and delivered to customers in 1891.

Armand Peugeot meanwhile had built his first light car, one that was a mechanical success from the start. Its 2½ hp rear-mounted Daimler engine, by now well-proved, took it on a safari trip following a cycle-race of some 2,415 km (1,500 miles) around France, at an average of 16 km/h (10 mph), the first such 'regularity' journey ever attempted in a motor vehicle.

Within a couple of years there were sufficient motor cars – and *auto-mobilistes* in France – for the newspaper *Le Petit Journal* to set up a contest. This time, said its editor Pierre Giffard, the event was not to be a cycle-race, but a test for automobiles, the first ever to be held. The cars were to be conducted from Paris to Rouen and the winners, not necessarily those who arrived first, but 'the vehicles that proved that

Peugeot with a fringe on top, 1895. This is a similar model to the Peugeots that took part in the first motor contest, the Paris to Rouen reliability trial of 1894.

Left : Panhard et Levassor, c. 1896, using the Daimler-licensed vertical-twin engine. This one may be seen at the Musée Nationale des Techniques in Paris.

This early De Dion poster tries hard to illustrate just about everything the company made in 1899. Shown here are a Model D voiturette (in the foreground), two tricycles and a steam bus.

Left : The French Hurtu company (1896–1929), like several other car-makers, progressed from sewing machines, to bicycles, to cars. This 1896 three-wheeler was based on the Bollée voiturette.

they could be handled without danger, were easily controlled, and economical to run.' Giffard had a good reason for stating this. He had recently accepted the offer of a friend to take him in his motor carriage to the scene of an incident – and had lost his news story through the abysmal unreliability of the machine. Giffard hoped to stimulate an interest in the machines as useful transportation, rather than the play-things of an eccentric band of sportsmen.

It seems hardly necessary to state that the prizes were divided between Messieurs Panhard et Levassor, and Les Fils de Peugeot, whose performances were infinitely more reliable than most of the puffing and panting steam engines. This event quickly brought the petrol vehicle to the attention of a wider and more informed public.

The following year they decided to make it a race from Paris to Bordeaux and back, a distance of 1,178 km (732 miles). Émile Levassor won handsomely in his own machine, carving his name in motoring history – and opening the gates to a new exciting sport.

Thus in France and in Germany motoring was, by the last years of the 19th century, a recognized sport, if not a genuine method of travel-ling from one place to another. In Britain, however, the horse and the railroad still shared the work of transport, and motored road travel was still, in effect, illegal. It remained so until November 1896, when the shackles of restrictive legislation were loosened a little if not completely struck off.

In the United States by 1896 there were large numbers of back-yard engineers forging and grinding their way into the automotive world, many following Benz principles of construction and engine design. Although hampered by the lack of technical knowledge crossing the Atlantic, competing against better-established steam and electric interests, and discouraged by the very absence of roads on which to use their ironworks engineering, they were a hardy bunch, and nothing was going to stop them.

Headlines in the periodical *Scientific American* in its January 1893 issue referred to the Benz car with enthusiasm: 'A marvellous motor – the new propelling power that has come out of poetic Germany – it is

The most popular power unit in Europe at the turn of the century was the 1¾-hp single-cylinder De Dion Bouton tricycle engine.

Ford's first vehicle, 1896. The orange-box body was supported by bicycle suspension; the thing had no brakes, no reverse and no steering wheel – but was to become the foundation for the vast Ford 'empire'.

Frank and Charles Duryea had tested their first car in 1893 at Springfield, Massachusetts. Two years later Frank established the first American company to make gasoline automobiles. This is an 1895 model.

independent of rails, and can fly over country roads at 30 miles an hour – the ride of Emperor William – no noise, no smoke, no steam, no odor – anyone can handle it' – and so on in a highly non-technical eulogy. Its first article on the new motoring, harbinger of the new mechanical age would, thought the magazine, put America at the head of the world's industry once it had got the hang of it all.

Already the brothers Frank and Charles Duryea were building their own car – something that borrowed from both Benz and Daimler – and indeed by 1893 its first test run had been accomplished at Springfield, Massachusetts. The next year Elwood Haynes, helped by the Apperson brothers, made a single-cylinder light car at Kokomo, Indiana. A year later, the *Chicago Times Herald*, hearing of *Le Petit Journal*'s Paris-Bordeaux race, sponsored one of its own, held eventually in November 1895 under the most appalling conditons of snow and ice. The result was somewhat inconclusive, but the race gave another sharp boost to those in America who were taking up the cause of motor travel in an age when the steamship and the railroads were still the backbone of long-distance travel and the horse the only practical power for day-to-day journeys and haulage.

With four years to go before the turn of the century, farmer's boy Henry Ford entered the stage. Down in the toolshed at his modest home in Bagley Avenue, Detroit, he was bolting together a crude boxlike quadricycle. At the kitchen sink on Christmas Eve 1893 he had already proved that his little gas-pipe-and-wire engine would work. Now it was installed in his first vehicle. Henry had to knock down his toolshed door to get it out – but once on the road it ran, a magic carpet that was to take Henry into the annals of history. When Ford tested his first car in Detroit the automobile was almost unknown in America. Ten years later its manufacture had become one of the most significant industries the world had seen.

To the Manner Born

The 12th of November 1896 closed the doors on the horse age in Britain, as with a snort of exhaust fumes the new motoring era commenced. Everyone who was anyone in the autocar motor automobile world (the name of the vehicles had not yet been settled) piled into their motored phaetons, dog-carts, tricycles, spiders, sociables, barouches (and one parcels van) and made a beeline for Brighton down on the coast. This was a day to remember! At last the brakes were off and British motorists could scorch along the rolling roads of England at a flying 12 mph.

Blazoned *The Autocar*, the country's first motor magazine: 'Today is a red-letter day, not only in the history of automobilism, but in that of England itself, for it marks the throwing open of the highways and byways of our beautiful country to those who elect to travel thereupon in carriages propelled by motors instead of horse-drawn vehicles or upon bicycles.'

The 'Emancipation Run' as it was called was watched by a huge crowd along the route. There were not sufficient cars in Britain at the

Still in rally trim – this 1895 one-cylinder Benz is seen speeding down the Brighton Road on a Commemoration Run.

22

time to mount a real show, so the organizers invited several French owners to swell the numbers. Even Gottlieb Daimler came, in a covered barouche of his own manufacture – and was the only entrant to arrive in Brighton reasonably dry.

The Run was intended to be a procession, but when the leading 'pilot' Panhard boiled and stopped, the day developed (no doubt because of those exuberant French drivers, said many) into something of a race. Chaos was universal, and there never was any coherent report of the event. Rumour had it that certain vehicles arrived in Brighton suspiciously early (were they put aboard a train?) and that a Duryea which was involved in a small accident somehow arrived at the finish without a mark, giving rise to the unkind thought that another identical machine was waiting on the route to take over. However a remarkably good time was had by all, and the great Brighton Run is still annually commemorated, to the delight of some 2 million spectators who never seem to tire of watching the old pioneer vehicles.

The dusty roads of Britain in the first years of the century provided little encouragement to motoring. Loose stones used for repairing surfaces originally intended for leisurely horse traffic, were dislodged and sprayed about the roads by faster-travelling motor cars. Columns of white dust heralded the approach of the car; brown cows turned

A Daimler wagonette, of 1897, seen here on the London-Brighton Run. It is typical of several vehicles that took part in the 1900 Thousand Miles Trial.

23

white and washing on the line became grey at its passing. Speeding too, although speeds were now at a legal maximum of 12 mph in most regions, was frowned upon by the police and there were many fines for scorching along over the limit, a figure calculated by a team of two constables strategically positioned in the hedgerows along a country road, who would signal a third officer stationed further along the road to stop the offender.

Tyres were a major problem. A trip of 30 miles could result in a puncture in each wheel. Repairing the tyre meant stripping off the beaded-edge cover, patching the holes or tear in the tube and replacing the lot, usually with some digital abrasions. When detachable rims were first seen in 1906 they were immediately put into service on racing vehicles, saving significant minutes of tyre repairing and winning races for the entrants who were first to use them. Dress was of prime importance too, when in (then the term was 'on') a motor car. The lack of windscreen, doors, hood or side protection meant that special clothing was vital – heavy fur or rubber capes in inclement weather, or long cloth coats to take the worst of the dust in summer. Ladies wore grotesque hats and masks to preserve their delicately pale complexion from the elements.

The cars themselves were often thirstier for water than for petrol, which was usually found – when it could be found – at an ironmonger, or a chemist's shop, or sometimes in conical-topped cans at an enterprising blacksmith's establishment. The vast quantities of spares to be carried included hatchets, spades, emergency rations and a few bottles of hock, as well as the more traditional repairing tools.

An early taxicab from the Cannstatt Daimler works. Gottlieb Daimler opened his 'Motor Carriage Hire Depot' in Stuttgart in 1896.

Right: 'No motor car is complete without a Patchquick equipment' it says on the box, and in a time when a morning's spin often resulted in a couple of punctures – it made sense!

Below: Motoring tourists in the U.S.A., 1905. The Rambler (this is a twin-cylinder Type 1 four-seater) was a popular car in its day. Total sales for 1905 were 3,807.

At first, few people in Great Britain were remotely interested in the car. Not many thought it had much of a future. Those who had taken up this bizarre way of travelling were bold, unconventional – and usually wealthy. Some of them had invested in the new industry started by pioneers like George and Fred Lanchester (first production car 1900) and in firms like the Wolseley Sheep Shearing Co. of Birmingham, or the new Daimler Motor Syndicate, and were determined that the populace should get more closely acquainted with motor transport. They decided to stage a motor tour of Britain – a Thousand Miles Trial.

Sixty-five cars took part in the marathon drive of April-May 1900, from London to the West Country, up through the Midlands to Manchester and the Lakes, over to Newcastle, York, Leeds, Sheffield, and back down to England through Nottingham to London's Marble Arch – no mean test of a car even today. And when one reads that Lord Montagu's 1899 Daimler, one of the most superior vehicles on the trial, had brake pads of wire-rope which tended to burn on application until dowsed, and that several cars had no radiators, replenishing water from tanks carried on the car, and that not a single vehicle had a windscreen – one wonders at the endurance of drivers who were after all, more accustomed to an occasional outing with gun or horse than this prolonged exposure to the elements.

Right: Wolseley, by Austin. Before he left the company, Austin designed this horizontal two-cylinder 10-hp tonneau.

Many new enterprises had sprung up during the last years of the 19th century, and 1899 saw the birth of several motor-manufacturing companies of significance. In France Louis Renault built his first car, made his first sale, and formed his first company in 1899. He went on to be showered with honours within a decade, as France's leading captain of industry, and his company continued to flourish until it grew so large that it became part of the national fabric of France itself.

In Italy a young cavalry officer had been tinkering with an old internal combustion engine, and by 1899 had bought a Storeo tricycle, and had won a race. Giovanni Agnelli found a group of willing businessmen, formed a company, F.I.A.T., in Turin – and went into production with a small 5-hp car of rather Victorian appearance, made in a little local factory they had bought from a cycle company. Fiat went on to become the industrial backbone of a newly industrialized Italy with interests in a dozen other industries, and itself the largest company of any kind in the land.

In the United States motor-manufacturing activity was also stirring. Like France in pre-gasoline-engine days, America had shown a strong

Right: A year after opening for business Louis Renault had built the world's first saloon, and this 3-hp watercooled light car.

*In 1899 young
Giovanni Agnelli
formed the motor
company
Fabbrica Italiana
di Automobili
Torino, later
known as Fiat.
This is their first
advertisement.*

Ford formed the Ford Motor Co. in 1903, with just 12 investors, $28,000 capital, tools, blueprints, a couple of models and an old converted wagon-works on Detroit's Mack Avenue. The first car, 'so simple a boy of 15 can run it', actually sold to a doctor, much to the relief of the stockholders who were keeping a worried eye on the remaining company bank balance of $223. The stock increased, as did the production, over the next years so that two of the original investors who had put in $5,000 apiece cashed in their shares some years later for over $12 million each!

The third man, Lansing machinist Ransom Eli Olds, had built a steamer in 1886 and completed his first gas-powered car in 1894. His company made no less than 11 electric models for sale in 1900; as one director said disparagingly, Olds was 'chasing after strange electric gods' in pursuit of success. On the drawing board however was a small single-cylinder gasoline runabout which was to be marketed concurrently with the electrics. One of them just *had* to appeal to the public, they said at the Olds Motor Vehicle Company at Lansing, Michigan.

At 1.35 p.m. on 9 March 1901, someone at the factory yelled 'Fire'! Before long the whole factory was ablaze. James Brady, a young time-keeper, dashed into the flames and dragged out the experimental prototype of the runabout.

Much loved by the ladies of America, the Baker Electric was a 'town carriage'. Its ease of starting, its silence in use, and its gentle progression were designed to please the few lady drivers of the day. This is a 1905 model.

31

The Curved-Dash runabout was the only car saved from the conflagration, a fact that forced the company into a one-model policy. Ransom Olds described the incident years later as 'this blessed event' and indeed the Oldsmobile fortunes were founded on this (entirely accidental) fire, with the simple little $650 tiller-steered car with the toboggan dash selling in great numbers over the next few years. 'Nothing to watch but the road' was one of the slogans and it brought in 425 customers in 1901, rising steadily to 5,500 in 1904. The 'Merry Olds' assembly line became the first genuine mass-production system, predating Ford's Model T methods by several years.

In Europe, French vehicles powered by French engines had captured the market by the turn of the century. De Dion units (the company had been in business for two decades now) were used in well over a hundred different makes of car as well as in the little 'Ding-Dongs' as the British called the De Dion tricycles and light cars.

Panhard et Levassor were also selling in strength both on the Continent and in Britain in the early 1900s, the mainstay of their range a large 7-litre four-cylinder with coil-and-battery ignition – a development of the original Daimler Phoenix. A year later a true Panhard engine of two cylinders appeared, designed by Arthur Krebs, successor to Emile Levassor who had died after a motor racing accident in 1897. They were being sold to the British public through a London agent, C. S. Rolls & Co., run by the Hon. Charles Rolls. He desperately wanted to be able to sell a British car to the British public – but there simply was not such a vehicle to be found.

Some 200 miles north of Rolls' showroom in London, in Cook St., Manchester, 41-year-old crane-maker Henry Royce had just completed building a small car. On 1 April 1904 he pushed it out of his workshop, gave the starting handle a flip – and the car whispered into

The Curved-Dash Olds – the car that saved the Oldsmobile company when it was adopted as its only production model in 1901.

Right: High-wheelers designed specifically for the appalling roads of America were made, in some cases, until 1910. This 1902 Holsman was typical of the sort of vehicle needed for the muddy tracks between towns.

operation. Later when the Press was shown the first Royce car, their praise was unstinted. 'The Royce car makes all others sound like an avalanche of teatrays', said one scribe. 'No realization of driving propulsion . . . a feeling of being wafted through the landscape . . . remarkable silence . . .' said others.

The Hon. Charles heard about the car, and after some show of Northern reluctance, Royce agreed to allow Rolls to take his entire output of vehicles for sale through the London office. Two years later the company of Rolls-Royce was formed, and at the 1906 Motor Show the new company exhibited its first large car, the 40-50 hp. It had a six-cylinder engine of 7 litres and a four-speed overdrive gearbox. Its open touring body was embellished with aluminium paint, and the car dubbed 'The Silver Ghost'. It was by this fanciful title that the car was known for the 19 years of its magnificently successful production run. It rapidly became the accepted transport of crowned heads and national leaders, and its safari exploits, durability tests and endurance trials soon became woven into the history of transport. The claim to be 'The Best Car in the world' was not originally made by Rolls-Royce – that accolade was first given to the car and the company by its users. That first Silver Ghost is kept in the showroom in London and is still in excellent running condition.

While it is accepted that the Rolls-Royce car had no peers in 1904, a vehicle that had appeared one Spring morning three years earlier on the promenade at Nice in the South of France had shocked the infant motor industry to its cast-iron core.

Left: Introduced in 1901, the first Peugeot 'Bébé' had a 652-cc, single-cylinder engine and a De Dion-type bonnet. Many were imported into England.

Best-seller in Europe at the turn of the century, the lightweight De Dion-Bouton voiturette. This 1901 model had a 4½-hp rear-mounted engine.

Overleaf: The ubiquitous De Dion, here in the guise of family brake, used the long-famous De Dion axle system in which the rear axle was 'dead', i.e. separated from the drive shafts. It was used for many years on sports and racing cars.

Above: Similar
to the De Dion
voiturette in
several features,
this Prunel was
manufactured just
down the road
from the Puteaux
works and used a
variety of
proprietary
engines.

Left: Immediate
forerunner of the
first Mercedes,
this Daimler
Phoenix of 1899
housed one of the
first four-cylinder
engines.

Daimler had been developing the *Système Panhard*, of which at first he had thought little, during the last years of the 19th century, and now placed his engines at the front of his cars. The Cannstatt Daimler Phoenix of 1899 had been the first genuine sports-racing car designed to this layout. With a four-cylinder, 24-hp, 5-litre engine, it could touch 80 km/h (50 mph), and its honeycomb radiator, an innovation that attracted considerable sharp-eyed notice, promised a cooler and more efficient performance. The new sporting car was matched against the large Panhards and Mors of the day, but its design was not completely successful – the car was too short and too tall for stability. The 1900 Nice Week saw the two-seater racing version of the car, but this too needed development.

Daimler's Côte d'Azur agent based at Nice asked for a more sophisticated car to be built to his own specifications. Emile Jellinek guaranteed to sell the first run of about 35 if they could be produced quickly. Willi Maybach, formerly Daimler's collaborator and since Gottlieb's death in 1900 mainspring of the company, designed a new car with young Paul Daimler's help.

Unveiled at the Nice meeting the following year, 1901, it caused a sensation: the other towering iron-and-wood clad cars at the sporting gathering immediately appeared as out of date as a coach-and-four, while the low clean-lined car from Cannstatt, named 'Mercedes' in honour of Jellinek's young daughter (it also sounded more acceptable to Gallic ears than the somewhat Wagnerian tones of the name Daimler) captured total interest – and the victor's laurels – during the week's events.

The first of the 'new' Daimlers of 1901 were given the name Mercedes. At the Nice Spring Meeting of that year the Mercedes opened a new era of motoring with its dramatic technical advances.

Overleaf: A Rexette three-wheeler forecar of 1904, from the Birmingham/Coventry Rex company. With single cylinder and 5 hp, it has a seat for the passenger 'nearest the accident'.

39

54

designation letter T. The Model T ambled into history on 1 October 1908 – officially the 1909 model – and within months became the symbol of cheap reliable transportation throughout the United States.

The Model T collected love-hate anecdotes like a magnet. One story tells of how car-owners in a European town during the First World War preferred to wreck their cars rather than leave them to the advancing German army. One by one they drove them to a cliff and plunged them over into a river. One of the cars shook itself, and chugged on through the water and up the bank, stopping only when it hit a tree. It was of course a Model T – and the story is a genuine anecdote of wartime history. 'Tin Lizzie' was the name given to the

Left: Wolseley-Siddeley, 1906. Wolseley changed from horizontal- to vertical-engined vehicles under J. D. Siddeley. This 25-hp landaulette houses a 5 190-cc engine.

David Dunbar Buick made his first car in 1902. Dealer Billy Durant bought the company in 1903 and went on to found the General Motors Corporation. This is a 1910 Buick.

Model T by the English-speaking world, although it certainly did not deserve it. Long-lasting, light and strong due to the extensive use of vanadium and heat-treated steels wherever possible, it weighed just 1,200 lbs and had a 100-inch wheelbase, clearing the road by $10\frac{1}{2}$ inches.

The four-cylinder engine (some of them were made by the Dodge Brothers who later built cars of their own) gave 20 hp and had a detachable cylinder head, unusual then. The pedal-operated planetary transmission was simple (it had to be, used as it was from farms in Idaho to tea plantations in Borneo) and the car could run 20 miles on a gallon of fuel. The transmission system did, it was admitted, give a little trouble sometimes – when the driver cranked the starting handle, the car could run forward over him.

So great was the demand and so efficient the production at Ford's new plant at Highland Park, Detroit, that Model Ts were running off

Left: Lozier of Plattsburg, New York, had moved from steam to gasoline in 1905 and went on to become makers of one of the highest-quality cars in America. Both cars in the foreground are Loziers.

Overleaf: 'Hotting up' a Model T Ford was a favourite sport of many young Americans. This one has had the treatment and is left with just two bucket seats and a monocle windshield.

Napier was
Britain's first
motor company to
take a close
interest in motor
racing, with an
entry in the
Paris-Toulouse
event of 1900.
With six-cylinder
engines from
1903, Napier
scored many
sporting successes.

the lines at the rate of one every ten seconds by 1913. No single car in the history of the motor world has made such an impact as Ford's Tin Lizzie.

By 1914 Ford was making half of the nation's cars, employing a sixth of the nation's automotive labour force, and giving unimagined mobility at first to the workers of America, and shortly afterwards to the world.

Back in England Herbert Austin had opened a factory in Birmingham. He had left the Wolseley company in 1905 and while Wolseley went on to make solid vertical-engined cars designed by J. D. Siddeley, Herbert, who had objected to the Wolseley policy changeover from horizontal power units to vertical cylinders, offered his first Austin car to the public – a large ornate 25/30-hp *vertical*-engined product.

Over in the Sarthe region of France meanwhile the first genuine motor-racing Grand Prix was being staged at Le Mans in 1906 after the earlier Gordon Bennett Trophy series had run out of steam due to some irritating entry rules. The old town-to-town races run in the first few years of the century on open public roads had long been abandoned as too dangerous, and the Grand Prix at the Sarthe circuit (not the one used today) was a closed-road-race with proper pits, and stands for spectators. A Renault won that first abrasive two-day race in the heat of a French summer sun – and in a blinding spray of hot tar that had been laid to keep down dust.

Sport on the British mainland was yet unborn, with only the T.T. (a race for touring cars) held on the Isle of Man, which was autonomous in such matters, to interest British enthusiasts. Motor racing was prohibited on public roads, manufacturers were tepid in their interest, and sporting drivers would regularly vanish over the English Channel for their competitive exercise.

However, a generous English family decided to give Britain a gift – a motor-racing circuit. The Locke-Kings were blessed with great wealth; they owned Mena House, the most famous hotel in Egypt, and had other similar assets. Locke-King bought a site in Surrey in the South of England, laid a vast pear-shaped circuit on it – using 200,000

Right : Renault
1909 9-hp light-
delivery van, an
indestructible
vehicle that was
to be seen in
many countries.
This one was
originally a taxi.

THE VEHICLE RAYDYOT EQUIPMENT
ONG

C 832

Above: A 1909 family Fiat, still capable of travelling long distances without complaint. This model has a four-cylinder, 30-hp engine.

Left: King Alfonso of Spain was an early aficionado of the Hispano-Suiza. This 1912 Alfonso sports racing vehicle, named after the monarch, was a superbly engineered 3.7-litre vehicle developing 64 bhp.

tons of cement – and opened it for sporting contests in 1907, within nine months of starting construction work. Brooklands Motor Course brought Britain into motor sport and helped in no small way to publicize British motor cars. Competition between thoroughbred racing vehicles was laced with record-breaking attempts and races for sports cars of the type the public could purchase, and with which they could identify.

Brooklands, the world's first real motor-racing track, was shortly followed by several others, the most famous of which is still America's Indianapolis Motor Speedway. The first races in this great banked basin were held in 1909, and two years later the first international 500-mile event took place. The 500 series is still with us and the only years in which it did not take place were the war years. 'Indy' cars, powerful and large, have provided some tremendously dramatic racing – and some horrific multiple disasters – on this clockwork-style track, and it was not until 1965 that the laurels went to a British car, a Lotus driven by the then current world champion Jim Clark.

By 1910 motoring was well established as part of the daily world of commercial transportation. There were as many cars, vans and trucks on the roads as horses, and most of the established professional class possessed a motor car. The lobbying power of that section of society was undoubtedly responsible for the rapid improvement in road surfaces in Europe and Britain around this time. Bitumen was now widely used in place of unbonded macadam. Dust was banished on most main roads. Cobbles, blocks and pavé in cities began to be replaced by the new surfacing.

Vauxhall Prince Henry, 1914. Four litres, 75 mph, and the first genuine British sports car.

The mechanics of the cars were tidied up considerably with some of the copper spaghetti of oil-carrying pipes replaced by drilled galleries, or ducts. The two camshafts used to operate T-head engines were reduced to the single one needed in an L-head (with its valves all on one side), of the sort that were becoming general then.

Sports cars, the nearest definition of which is probably a motor car in which the road-holding and performance is of greater importance than the comfort of the passengers, first appeared in the period 1910–11.

In Barcelona, Spain, a young Swiss engineer, Marc Birkigt, had designed a car called the Castro. Renamed the Hispano-Suiza (Spanish-Swiss) in 1904, it was a finely engineered 20-hp four-cylinder vehicle. A couple of years later the cars were part of the motor stables of King Alfonso XIII – and by 1912 a racing voiturette named after the king was being bought by the *cognoscenti* of Europe, in sports version.

A young engineer, Laurence Pomeroy of the Vauxhall company of Luton, England, had designed a four-cylinder, 20-hp, 3-litre car which gave a creditable 38 hp at 2400 rpm. The car had won the 1908 2,000 Mile Trial, and made its mark in a number of other British events. In 1910 it put up a capable performance in the German *Prinz Heinrich* Trials. The Prince Henry Vauxhall became the first real British sports car, and by 1913 had developed into a 4-litre 75-hp vehicle, capable of 75 mph, and costing just £615. From 1911 on its competition achievements and class speed records were impressive, and led to a second-generation vehicle, the first of the Vauxhall 30/98 sports cars, which became a sporting legend during the 1920s as one of the finest in Europe, winning hundreds of competition honours – and still flexible enough to take the family out for a Sunday spin.

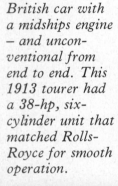

Lanchester, the British car with a midships engine – and unconventional from end to end. This 1913 tourer had a 38-hp, six-cylinder unit that matched Rolls-Royce for smooth operation.

Right: Bill Morris's first automotive offering was the Oxford of 1913. It has a 1018-cc, four-cylinder engine, two seats, and a top speed of around 55 mph.

*Above left :
British middle-
of-the-road. For
21 years
Waverley built
good solid motor
cars in North
London for solid
citizens. This is a
12/15-hp of
1914, worth
today many times
its original price
of £400.*

*Left: An
American visitor
to Shakespeare
country. This
air-cooled six-
cylinder
Franklin, vintage
1914, seems to
blend happily
with the half-
timbering of the
16th-century
manor house.*

Vauxhall's bold planning and rapid success encouraged many other British manufacturers to produce middle-range popular owner-drive cars – vehicles with few sporting aspirations perhaps, but directed to the newly emergent motoring public of the increasingly prosperous times just before the First World War. Bill Morris from Oxford was one of the newcomers to motor-making then – and he managed to turn his cycle-repair business into a vast motor empire. Leading the field in France was Louis Renault once again, although at this time the foremost French automobile producer was still attracted by the carriage-trade, and was producing 9-litre chassis-only examples, in addition to simple-bodied cars as small as 2 litres.

The United States, by now a powerful force in the automotive world, having opened the gates to a brand new public – the female section of society – by developing the electric self-starter and taking the hard labour out of swinging the engine, was making cars with all-steel bodies (first to appear, Oakland and Hupmobile), a factor which considerably reduced costs. The Dodge brothers were making their first car by 1914, a down-to-basics 25-hp open tourer; Chevrolet, too, was in production by 1911 with a car that was to become America's best-seller. Some of the electrics were still around, and steamers were not yet buried. The popular air-cooled Franklin still flourished and in fact had another 20 years to run before its demise.

The automotive world was, in 1914, squaring-up to becoming the world's largest manufacturing industry. U.S. production alone in 1914 was over 500,000, and the automobile itself had been developed to mechanical reliability undreamed of only half-a-dozen years earlier. The war that started in 1914 was only a minor hiccup in the relentless progress of this mammoth industry. In many ways it further stimulated its growth.

*Lozier of the
U.S.A. had
captured many
speed and racing
trophies in their
earlier days, but
sporting success
did not save them
from failing in
1917. This is a
1916 Lozier
Model 84, last of
the company's
products.*

The Open Road

The year is 1919, the time 8 a.m.; location, Hendricks, West Virginia. A young office worker finishes his breakfast, kisses his wife and leaves for the office. He climbs into his high-sided Model T Ford, sets the spark and throttle levers on the steering wheel at ten-to-three and descends to crank the engine. He is lucky, and the engine starts. It is a cold morning, the car might well have needed half-a-dozen hefty swings. The driver leaps quickly to the steering wheel and re-sets the spark and throttle levers at twenty-to-two.

Off with the handbrake, left foot on the low-speed pedal and as he gathers speed he lifts his foot to allow the car to change up into top. Cross-roads approaching – he brakes either with the reverse, or the low-speed pedal (or both) or punches all three pedals (including the 'official' brake pedal) one after the other. You could hardly fail to stop.

That could have been a fairly typical routine in 1919 for over two million Model T owners in the U.S.A. and no less than 750,000 more owners would join the morning ritual this year, as Model Ts poured off the lines at the great new Rouge factory.

America in 1919, comparatively untouched by the Great War, was already a car-owning nation. While the Peace Treaty with Germany was being signed at Versailles that June, there were already seven million passenger cars registered in the U.S.A.

From that year on the pattern of car design, ownership and – to a certain extent – usage, changed dramatically on both sides of the Atlantic.

America was to go towards the big car with the big engine, a route still travelled today, despite cries from Europe about gas-guzzlers and conservation; in Europe the trend would be towards smaller, more economical automobiles, down eventually to such tinies as the 500-cc Fiat 'Topolino'.

Left: A 1929 Duesenberg Model J. This car could produce 265 bhp (today's family car develops about 80 bhp), a figure claimed to be over twice as much as any other comparable American car. The one shown here has a 1937 body by Graber of Switzerland.

At the London Motor Show of 1919, a total of 134 British marques were listed – and despite a tough 33⅓ per cent duty on imported cars imposed during the war and then retained, 130 foreign manufacturers were ranged against them.

Cars were still big, and they were expensive. It was the day of the Rolls-Royce Silver Ghost, the sleeve-valve Daimler 30, the graceful and sporting Lanchester 40, the first hints of the Bentley (made in 1919 but not offered as a production model until 1921), the Sunbeam 16/40, the Crossley 4½ litre.

In France engineer André Citroën, who in 1914 had made his name with the manufacture of bevel gears on patents bought from Poland (the herringbone bevel is still Citroën's trademark) and who had made millions of shells for Allied guns during the World War, now turned his attention towards cars. When the *Salon de l'Automobile* opened in Paris

From Oshawa, Ontario, Canada, this 1920 McLaughlin was part-Buick, but of somewhat higher quality than the American car. After 1923 the name was changed to McLaughlin-Buick.

a month before the London Motor Show, Citroën was already building 35 cars a day. Believing firmly that Ford's mass-production methods were the only road to success, Citroën produced one model only: he launched his 1·3-litre Type A, the famous Torpedo, an open four-seater with pressed steel wheels and a top speed of 64 km/h (40 mph). It was modestly priced at Fr. 7,950 (about £320 then), and the Paris company was soon building 10,000 cars a year.

Citroën was quickly challenged by Renault, already with experience in manufacturing small cars. Renault went into production with a 1·3-litre four-cylinder model which had a similar success to that which the famous Citroën Deux-Chevaux was to realize a quarter century later.

The Lanchester 40 of 1919 had a six-cylinder, 6178-cc, front-mounted engine, and only two doors – both opening into the rear compartment!

However, as the Twenties dawned, a large number of European manufacturers were still building mammoth automobiles, although their design was considerably influenced (and improved) by wartime experience in tanks, trucks and aircraft engines.

One of the most outstanding of these designs, shown at the 1919 *Salon*, was the Hispano-Suiza 37·2-hp H6B. In 1916 the firm had built a V8 200-bhp aero engine to power the Spad fighter aircraft. Highest power for the lowest weight had then been the demand; from this stemmed a great 135-bhp six-cylinder engine with dual ignition, twin-choke carburettor, overhead camshaft and a significantly light alloy block with steel liners.

The H6B came with servo-assisted four-wheel brakes at a time when even Rolls-Royce were still relying on rear-wheel anchors only. Installed in a French-built chassis, the H6B was a sure-fire winner among the wealthy. One of its great claims to fame was its popularity

Right: The Singer Ten of 1912 was a 'big car in miniature', as the makers claimed, and continued in production with few changes after the First World War, in both family and sporting forms.

among novelists and other entertainers of the Twenties. Michael Arlen in his book *The Green Hat* described it like this:

'Open as a yacht, it wore a great shining bonnet, and flying over the crest of this great bonnet, as though in proud flight over the heads of scores of phantom horses, was the stork by which the gentle may be pleased to know that they have escaped death beneath the wheels of a Hispano-Suiza car, as supplied to His Most Catholic Majesty. . . .'

That really is writing about cars at the top of your voice.

Longer and heavier than the Hispano was the Isotta-Fraschini, also at the 1919 *Salon*. The Tipo 8 boasted an engine of 80 hp but lacked the power to match the Hispano's top speed of 145 km/h (90 mph).

The Rolls-Royce model of the day was still the six-cylinder 40/50 model, the Silver Ghost. In 1922, however, Rolls-Royce bowed to the wind of economic change and introduced a 20-hp (RAC rating) model of 50 bhp. Though somewhat underpowered, the 'Baby Rolls', as it was irreverently called, was a qualified success and continued in production up to 1929, during which time 3,000 were made.

Left: This exotically shaped car is a Horstmann, which in spite of its name and its appearance was built in Bath, England. This is the 1921 Super Sports, with Coventry-Simplex engine.

Rolls-Royce Silver Ghost power unit, 1921.

The 6·5-litre 12-cylinder Lancia also appeared in 1919, with two banks of cylinders inclined at a 22-degree angle in a single casting. Not surprisingly, this giant proved uneconomical to manufacture, but it paved the way to the innovative Lambda of 1922.

In the Lambda, Vincenzo Lancia built the first piece of road machinery with genuine integral construction, using deep pressed-steel side-members to form the structure of the open four-seater body. The Lambda also had a first-class four-wheel braking system, and sliding pillar independent front wheel suspension which made it cling to the road like a leech.

Peugeot offered a colossal nine-litre model while taking a stab at the 'street' market with a 760-cc Quadrilette, which had two seats in tandem. Later made as a side-by-side seater, the ungainly but fuel-saving Quadrilette had big sales in France and was sometimes considered the ancestor of the Austin Seven.

The Quadrilette was in fact a cyclecar, part of a short-lived development of both the late Edwardian period and the early 1920s. Produced because of shortages of materials and the consequent lack of 'real' cars, the cyclecar vogue nevertheless led to some interesting developments.

Overleaf: The entire car, vintage '22. A Rolls-Royce Silver Ghost, Derby-made, for the élite of motoring society.

Left: Austin's great workhorse, the Heavy 12/4, sometimes described as the 'hardest-wearing machine of all time', and one of Herbert Austin's most successful designs. This is the Clifton Tourer version.

The London-made sporting G.N. was one of these. The 1922 G.N. Vitesse was an air-cooled V-twin, with a capacity of 1087 cc and chain-drive. Built by H. R. Godfrey – later to build the famous H.R.G. sports car – and Captain 'Archie' Frazer-Nash – another sports car builder of the future – the G.N. had a charm of its own. W. H. Charnock, the motoring poet, summed up the G.N. like this:

Nash and Godfrey hated cogs,
Built a car with chains and dogs.
It worked, but would it if
They had made it with a diff?

In Germany the 'Kommisbrot' was built by Hanomag. With a 500-cc single-cylinder engine, it sold about 16,000 during the three years of production. Most cyclecars, though undeniably cheap to buy, were noisy and uncomfortable, combining – as one critic of the day put it – 'the comfort of a cement-mixer, the noise of a pneumatic drill and the directional stability of a chicken with its head off.'

Side by side with the cyclecar in Britain came the three-wheeler, of which the Morgan will always remain the best-loved. Harry Morgan launched his first commercial three-wheeler at the 1911 Motor Cycle Show; in 1912 he won the first-ever cyclecar race at Brooklands at an average speed of 57 mph.

By the 1920s, Morgans had grown into true automobiles (despite their two wheels at the front and one chain-driven wheel at the rear)

Left: High-quality engineering and longevity were the hallmarks of Alvis, who opened for business after the First World War. This is the ever-popular 12/50 sports tourer of 1927.

A lightweight from France, the Salmson developed from a simple cyclecar-type vehicle to a serious sporting participant. This is a 1921 car – obviously stripped down for sport, although the lady is in the height of fashion.

Overleaf: A name to conjure with; the Minerva in its early days was the choice of those who wanted refinement allied to performance. This is the 1926 AK32/34 of that prominent Belgian marque.

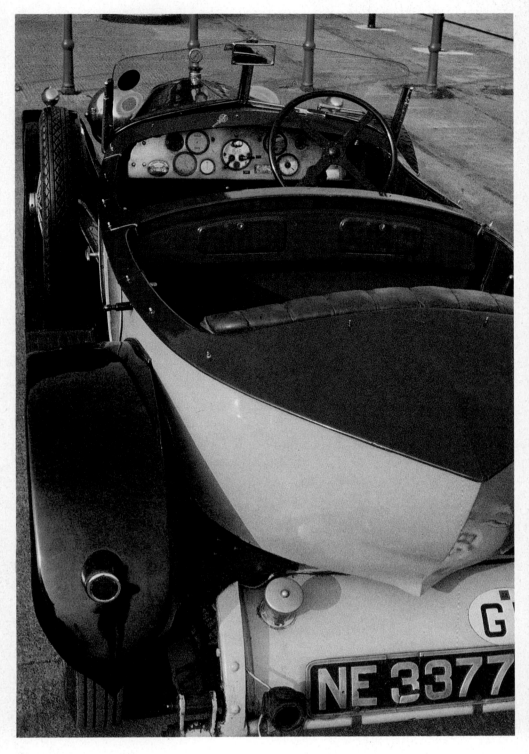

with proper all-weather equipment and car-type controls.

The 1920s saw a rebirth of motor sport, with England's Brooklands becoming the premier race circuit in Europe. At the same time road-circuit racing regained its popularity, and tremendous battles were staged between the 2-litre Sunbeams and the Delage V-12s, Sunbeam themselves having merged with Talbot and Darracq in 1920, a move which gave them exceptional strength in competition.

Meanwhile Ettore Bugatti built his beautiful Type 35 – two litres, eight cylinders in-line, exhaust valves larger than the inlets, front springs passing through the hollow front axle . . . it was a jewel of unorthodox design. Between 1924 and 1927 it won 1,851 races, and any amateur could buy it from the showroom for just over £1,000.

Of all the sporting machinery built in the Racing Twenties, the superb Bentley has earned its place in history. Between 1923 and 1930, Bentleys won the Le Mans 24-Hour Race five times. In 1927 two 3-litre and one 4·5 were leading when a multiple crash involved all three. Londoner S. C. H. ('Sammy') Davis, in the last 3-litre, buckled the car's front wheel, bent the front axle, smashed two of the three head-

Above left: Derived from the 2·1-litre DI of 1914, this 1925 Delage DISS Boat-Tail tourer is a classic example of the distinguished French sportif marque.

Above: Fiat were concerned with luxury machines in addition to bread-and-butter cars. This 519S (six cylinders, 4.8 litres, and servo-assisted brakes) was the smaller version of the upper-bracket V12 Super Fiat.

Left: Avant *Traction Avant. The Citroën B14G of 1928, all-steel bodywork, 1·5 litres and rear-wheel drive, was the French company's best seller that year.*

Above left: A
1926 Bentley
3/4·5-litre Le
Mans two-seater
Speed Model –
still able to
challenge its peers
on the circuit
today.

Left: This 1922
Belsize-
Bradshaw (9-hp,
two-stroke
engine) has a
claim to fame –
its engine was oil-
cooled and much
quieter than most.

lights and considerably altered the rest of its structure. The other two cars were write-offs.

'Sammy' nursed the car back to the pits and set to work repairing it. In 1927 the regulations banned anyone from helping the driver make repairs.

Within half an hour the Bentley was running and back in the race. With his co-driver, Dr. J. D. Benjafield, Davis continued through the night in pouring rain, fought back up to third position and then, 40 minutes from finish, rammed 'Old No. 7' into the lead, and held it there. In 24 hours that battered Bentley had averaged 100 km/h (62 mph), to win the race and create one of the legends of sporting history.

W. O. Bentley had produced his first 3-litre in 1921, and a total of 1,600 cars were made; Short Standard, Long Standard, Tourist Trophy Replica, Light Tourer, Speed Model and 100-mph Model. During the years that followed, along came the 4·5-litre, the 6·5-litre, the 'Speed Six' and the mammoth 8-litre; the 4·5-litre models with superchargers – the 'Blower Bentleys' – would hit 130 mph at full chat. Ettore Bugatti may have said: 'I have the greatest respect for Mr. Bentley. He builds the strongest and fastest lorries in the world.' But 'W.O.' certainly knew how to make them go!

Alfa-Romeo was another challenger in the great racing seasons of the Twenties. The Type P2, designed by Nicola Romeo, was an eight-in-line 2-litre machine with room for driver and racing mechanic, giving 170 bhp and a top speed of 225 km/h (140 mph). It was fast enough in 1924 to win the World Championship, leading to Alfa's development in 1927 of the 1·5-litre ohc six-cylinder 'Turismo' with such advanced features as a fan driven by the camshaft through a friction clutch.

In turn, this led to the supercharged Tipo 6C model, a hairy sports car indeed. Giulio Ramponi, mechanic turned driver, pushed this to first place in the 1929 'Double Twelve' at Brooklands, covering 1,824 miles at an average speed of 122 km/h (76 mph).

The Jowett 7-hp
'Short Two' two-
seater of 1923
has a two-
cylinder
horizontally
opposed unit.
'Cheerful and
long-lasting' was
the general
opinion, and not
much to fall off.

A year later the 17/85 1·75-litre cars appeared – the 'Gran Turismo' and 'Gran Sport' supercharged models. With a body by Italian coach-builder Zagato, the 1750 cc 'Gran Sport' is one of the prettiest cars of the period, capable of 0–97 km/h (0–60 mph) in 10 seconds and a top of 153 km/h (95 mph).

For the ordinary motorist, mass-production, long accepted in the States, was now bringing to Europe the smaller, cheaper car. Though a British importer was still selling the Stanley 735-A steam car in 1920, potential buyers were looking at cars like the 11·9 hp AC of 1921, with zip-fastened sidescreens, three-speed gearbox mounted on the rear axle (and a transmission brake, which was its only means of stopping), or the 10·8-hp Clyno, powered by a Coventry-Climax engine, or an 8-hp Humber Chummy.

In 1920–21, Morris – having launched both the Oxford and the Cowley in 1913 and 1915, respectively – was almost caught by a post-war recession. Sales plummetted from 288 in October 1920 to 68 in January 1921. Morris promptly cut the price of the Cowley four-seater from £525 to £425 and slashed other models by amounts from £25 to £90. Both his sales and his profits rose; the great era of the family motor-car for Britain was under way at last.

Herbert Austin, already a manufacturer of cars ranging from 12 to 20 hp (the 1921 '20' was a four-cylinder of 3601 cc and a bhp around 55), brought out his 'Seven' in 1922. Said to have been designed on his billiard table at home, it was actually his second Seven, the first being a pre-war single-cylinder of Swift parentage. At first the public considered the Seven a 'toy' car and there were jokes about 'wearing an Austin Seven on each foot'... but the price of £165 and the reliability of this (almost) four-seat, fully-equipped car soon spread its fame.

Herbert Austin's masterpiece. The Seven of the early Twenties was the butt of public laughter at first but soon proved the most popular small car in Britain. This one is a restoration based on a derelict found in an orchard some years ago.

A challenge to both the Cowley and the Seven was the plodding ever-faithful chain-drive Trojan. With a two-speed epicyclic gearbox, its four-cylinder, two-stroke engine was said to have only seven moving parts. The cylinders were arranged in a square, each pair sharing a common combustion chamber and a long, V-shaped con-rod which, instead of articulating as the pistons moved up and down, simply flexed itself!

Because of its low price (£125 in 1925) the 1529-cc Trojan became known as the 'clergyman's car'; like the mills of God, they said, it ground slowly, but surely.

Thus, the era of the common (motoring) man had truly arrived. Cars were now for everyday use, not merely for sport, leisure or adornment, and by the time the 1920s slid into the 1930s and the years of the Great Depression, the automobile had become a symbol of the middle class.

The Trojan 10-hp Utility, with two-stroke, flat-four engine that clattered away under the floor. A good hill-climber and load-puller, it was worthy of its name. Its German parallel was the equally basic Hanomag 'Kommissbrot'.

83

Duesenberg designs were built and sold by E. L. Cord from 1926, when he bought the company. Cord owned the old-established Auburn firm, as well as the Lycoming aircraft engine company. The 150-bhp boat-tail supercharged Auburn Speedster came with a guarantee of 100 mph. With two silver exhausts emerging from the engine housing and a sharply-raked V-style windshield, it was the typical playboy car of its generation.

The Cord 810 of 1935, designed by Gordon Buehrig, drew acclaim from all sections of the public. It was low-slung, with an alligator bonnet and wrap-round front wings which held disappearing head-lights. Power came from a 4·7-litre V8 Lycoming with alloy heads and a dual-choke Stromberg carburettor. With independent front sus-pension and a Bendix electric gearbox, it was a designer's dream. But even with the introduction of the supercharged 100-mph '812' a year later, only 2,300 cars were sold, and the Cord empire's demise was not far off.

In Europe the trend was still towards smaller cars, dictated by the world-wide depression. During the first five months of 1931, sales in Britain of over-10-hp cars fell by more than 10,000 compared with the previous year; at the same time, under-10-hp car sales rose by 2,000.

Wrote Sir Percival Perry, chairman of Ford in Britain: 'The tendency everywhere is to buy smaller and cheaper motor cars.' In October 1931 designers put an 8-hp Ford on the drawing-board. Within four months 16 prototypes were on the road, even the great Henry himself, at 67, using a spanner to help build them. The Model Y emerged at Ford's own London Motor Show with a proposed price of £120, and within a year Dagenham had built 32,958 of the famous 'Ford Eight' saloons.

Morris promptly brought in a similar 8-hp model, offering hydraulic brakes and a chassis which would take open bodywork. Ford of Britain quickly reduced the Y trimmings to a minimum and cut the price in rapid stages to £115, £110 and then – in 1935 – to the magic £100, the first time a fully-equipped four-seater saloon had been offered at this price.

For the first time, too, motoring was within the reach of the two-up, three-down houseowner (a modest home could be bought for £600 then), and in 1935 Ford's share of the small-car market rose to 41 per cent, giving the company more than 22 per cent of the total British market.

The Fiat Balilla, of which 113,000 were sold between 1932 and 1937, began as a workaday car, acquired sporting qualities, and by 1936 dominated the 1100-cc sports-car racing class. While the production model climbed somewhat tardily to 97 km/h (60 mph), the winner of the production class in the 1933 Mille Miglia had averaged a creditable 87 km/h (54 mph) throughout.

Citroën's brilliant Traction Avant, the first popular-production front-wheel-drive car, was a huge success when launched in 1934. In France the long low Citroën with its dashboard gear-shift was seen everywhere – always in grey or black – and became a coveted symbol of French advanced technology.

Opel with 31 per cent of the German export market (and the largest automobile manufacturer in the country) was in trouble. Domestic sales had declined sharply through short-sighted government tax policy. The coming depression cast its shadow.

Russelsheim-based Opel was acquired by General Motors in January 1929, and that year saw the company's first 8-cylinder model, the Regent. The Laubfrosch of the Twenties was developed into

U.S. style-setter. The Cord 810 housed a Lycoming V8 under its sphinx-like hood. With its wrap-round grille, retractable headlights, and a score of advanced internal mechanics, it acquired a mystique that still clings.

Right: Jeep in wartime uniform. The all-terrain utility of the Second World War was the final development of plans that started as far back as 1918, but the Jeep as we know it was born in 1940 when a quarter-ton, four-wheel-drive, low-profile vehicle was needed by the U.S. Army.

Below: Citroën Traction Avant, the front-wheel-drive saloon that was the French company's greatest success. Launched in 1934, the 7cv car bristled with innovations.

The Vauxhall T-Type Hurlingham open sports was one of very few true sports cars made by the Luton, England, company after amalgamating with General Motors. With boat-tail rear and dual cowl, it was a car for Continental travel – the last of the Vauxhalls built in the 30/98 idiom.

several small models, and the Kapitan, Olympia, and six-cylinder Admiral completed a large range of popular cars in the Thirties.

The British success story was certainly that of Jaguar. The original company, Swallow Sidecars, had gained experience in building specialist bodies for Austin, Morris, Swift, Fiat and Wolseley; in 1931 it launched the SS1, a car based largely on Standard Motor Company components.

Using much of the machinery from the bigger Standards, 'Bill' Lyons put his SS1 on the market, a rakish coupé with a bonnet that seemed to stretch forever, and seats which were publicized as 'like sitting in your armchair at home.'

From this sprang the SSII, a 1-litre version, and later the SS90, a six-cylinder side-valve sports car which managed only a somewhat dubious performance. Quickly this was developed into the 3·5-litre 124-bhp SS100, a strong attraction for the sports car fan with its genuine 100 mph and thoroughbred look – all for £445. The Jaguar name, in association with SS, was used as early as 1935, but became a

marque name only after the Second World War when the name of the Coventry company was changed to Jaguar Cars Ltd. in 1945.

Though the MG had been in production since 1924, it was introduction of the Morris Eight which really led this marque to become the most-loved of all British sports cars. The car served as a basis for the MG Midget, the car which scored the first real successes in motor sport. The M-type Midget of 1928 housed an 847-cc ohc engine which gave about 20 bhp at 4,000 revs, mounted in a rather dull boat-shaped body, and was followed by the C-type Midget (44 bhp at 6,000 rpm from 746 cc). In its Montlhery version it looked almost like a real racing car ... and it persuaded the customers to think that way.

Of all the Midgets, however, the J2 of 1932-34 is the most affectionately remembered. Stark and menacing, with cycle-type wings and fold-flat windshield, this was the young man's dream car of the Thirties, and its engine note was the song of its era.

Although Ford of Britain scored its greatest successes with the Model Y designed for the impecunious family man, and the 1172-cc Ten first seen in 1935 (in trials and rallies it became a firm favourite), Ford also developed the sales of the Model A which, because of their small bore could be taxed as 14·9-hp cars. From these derived the Model B, offered either as a 14·9 or 30-hp four cylinder. London's police used the 14·9 for some years, converting the steel roof into a leather-covered hard top which housed an aerial for the Morse-transmitting cop who sat in the rear seat.

Despite the fact that they drew a crippling 25 shillings-per-horse-power tax, the big American-type 30-hp Ford V8s were also exceptionally popular because of their smoothness and speed. From 1936 there was a smaller version, the 22 hp (2·2 litres and 60 bhp) which in saloon form would touch 75 mph; most of these were converted into ambulances and fire-trucks at the beginning of the Second World War.

Then as Ford introduced their 1939 Prefect, a 10-hp saloon at £185, the dogs of war were ready once more to slip their leashes.

Above left: British traditional. Armstrong-Siddeley cars were distinguished by their solid comfort, impeccable workmanship and driving stability. This is a 20-hp Burlington of 1935, in suitably orthodox environment.

Above: The U.S.-designed Ford Models A and T were the only Fords to be made in Britain until 1932. This is a smart two-seater Model A.

Left: The MG Midget was made from 1929 to 1932 and challenged the highly successful Austin Seven in its two-seater form. Early Midgets used the current Morris Minor 847-cc unit and were clothed in fabric-covered plywood.

The Years of Austerity

After six years of war there were no new cars. You went into the dealer's showroom, cap in hand, and asked politely if you could put your name down for the possible purchase of a new model, if and when it was ever produced.

Since 1939, the only new cars built for the owner market had been a few Hillman Minxes, produced specially in 1943 for customers who could persuade the authorities that it was essential that they had transport. Those who qualified were some doctors, war workers and precious few others.

There *were* cars to be found, of course, but few of them were bargains. A 1937 B.S.A. 10-hp saloon, with umpteen thousands on the clock, would fetch £150. A KN Magnette, burning clouds of oil and knock-kneed at the front end, fetched perhaps £175. The Ford Anglia you had sold in 1942 for £30 because you did not have space to keep it up on blocks 'for the duration' was offered back to you for £150 and a 1938 Rover 10 was listed at £685 in 1949.

Yet, as far as the rest of Europe was concerned, Britain was lucky. Germany had no cars at all. France and Belgium were running on pre-war Peugeot 401Ds and Opel Kadetts.

In Britain, on 3 September 1939, this edict had been issued: 'To meet the present emergency, Petrol Distributors throughout the

The only cars for private ownership built during the war were a handful of Hillman Minxes for essential use.

Early post-war Ford. British-made V8s had been available before the war and continued almost unchanged from 1947 to 1950 under the name of Pilot.

country have arranged to pool all their resources. No further supplies of individual brands will be made to Garages and Service Stations and in the interests of essential national economy, one grade of Motor Spirit only will be supplied for resale to the public. This will be called POOL Motor Spirit.'

It stayed like that until the night of Saturday, 31 January 1953. For those 14 years driving was rationed, allowing a maximum of 200 miles a week, until 1942, when *all* leisure motoring ceased, with essential users fighting for their 'E' (Essential) coupons. By the time Pool was swept away, the price of petrol had risen to three shillings (15p) a gallon, and it included a petrol tax of one shilling and six pence (7½p).

In 1945 the cheapest car in Britain was the (pre-war designed) Ford Anglia at £293, including £64 purchase tax. Soon after that it was possible to see Triumph 1800 roadsters in the showrooms; basically a three-seater, the 1800 had possibilities for two more passengers in the boot (a relic of the 'dickey' or 'rumble' seat), and was powered by an ohv version of the Standard 14, the company which now owned Triumph. This engine, by the way, also turned up in Jaguar's smallest car of the same period.

Riley came along with a new shape in the form of the 1·5-litre saloon, using a pre-war engine design, but with some very fine new suspension and road-holding qualities. The Jowett Javelin, however, was one of the first true post-war cars. With a flat-four engine of 1·5 litres, the 1947 Javelin was a brilliant piece of motor engineering for its

time, capable of reaching 80 mph. It soldiered on until the middle 1950s with little change in the specification when the even more sophisticated sporting Jupiter joined the Jowett stable.

Bentley (a Rolls-Royce by any other name) produced a new Mark VI model in 1946, based on the Mark V produced in 1939-40. Standard continued with variations of the Flying series, and the 8-hp saloon was a winner; then, in 1948 they adopted a one-model policy and built the rugged Vanguard, a 2-litre saloon which sold internationally as well as in Britain.

Triumph followed their early roadster with the 1800 saloon, known as the Renown, a razor-edge body design using the Vanguard engine and chassis. They then went into the smaller car market and introduced the 10-hp Mayflower, also a razor-edge, which was sound but too heavy for its power unit.

With the war over, American industry was given permission to build 200,000 cars for the rest of 1945 – and almost simultaneously informed by the government that prices for automobiles should be restricted.

Henry Ford II commented acidly: 'It costs us $1,041 to make a car ... but we are restricted to selling it at a maximum of $780.' While a survey of American motorists in 1945 indicated that most wanted plain-finished four-door sedans in black, light grey or dark blue, what they got, take it or leave it, was the 1946 automobile, with a shark's grin at the front, more fins than any fish could boast, and a weight of

The 'razor-edge' Triumph Renown of 1950, prestige model of the marque. With aluminium panels on an ash frame and a 1·8-litre engine of the type originally made for the 1·5-litre Jaguar, the Renown was introduced in 1946.

99

chrome that must have severely increased its fuel consumption. One New York motoring writer wrote:

'The grille has been further widened and lessened in height. The bumper is more massive and wraps further round the front wheels. Alas, the effect is more and more like some nightmare creature coming up for air from a thousand fathoms!'

Everybody wanted to build cars. Mathis, the Strasbourg car manufacturer who had fled to America when the Germans occupied France, planned a car using plastics and weighing less than its five passengers. It did not materialize. Henry J. Kaiser, who had built Liberty ships and almost everything else for the war effort, now launched the Kaiser-Frazer with aluminium engine and swivelling headlights that were supposed to follow the road. It sold to only five per cent of the market in 1948 and then disappeared.

Automatic transmission was now the norm, and names like 'Hydramatic', 'Powerglide' and 'Miracle H-Power' abounded. But the American car, if gaudy in appearance and sloppy on corners, came with all the trappings of the post-war world: V8 engines in the main, sealed-beam headlights, radio, heater, and engineering that included independent helical suspension at the front end. If you really wanted manual gearchanging (a fun-box) it often cost more.

Greatest success of the post-war period was the Volkswagen. Dr. Porsche's little 'Beetle' has been sold to over 15 million motorists since the factory reopened in 1945.

So-called compact cars arrived on the American market late in the decade, when Oldsmobile and Buick introduced their 'smaller' models, with V8 3·5-litre engines and a length of nearly 16 feet. The same engine was, a few years later, adapted for the Rover in Britain.

Creating a car to suit popular demand had a fortunate result for the Germans. Hitler had long ago decreed that there should be a car outside every German home, and Dr. Ferdinand Porsche had produced the first true Volkswagen design in 1934. The price, said the Führer, must not be more than £50, the car should be able to cruise at 100 km/h (60 mph), have four seats and run at 40 mpg. It should also have an air-cooled engine because only the wealthy owned warm garages.

Now, some 12 years later, the real Volkswagen was getting into its stride – though early designs were in war-time use as the Wehrmacht's Kubelwagen, and the amphibious Swimmwagen. Launched into limited production at the Wolfsburg factory in 1945, the VW was first offered to various Allied car manufacturers. Said the British: 'This car does not

Taking the sheep to market. One, perhaps, in the Citroën 2cv, designed before the Second World War but unseen until 1949, when it captured a large market. Originally powered by a tiny 375-cc unit, it was often described as a garden shed on wheels. This is a Seventies example.

101

fulfil the technical requirements which must be expected from a motor car' – and rejected it as a viable commercial proposition. However the Beetle went on to become the most popular model of all time, continuing in production for more than 40 years, and VW supplied the world's public with more cars than any other manufacturer in automotive history – including Ford's prodigious 15 million Model T sales.

Of almost equal success was the 2cv Citroën – an 8-bhp flat-twin of 375 cc, with corrugated slab-sided bodywork and a foldback canvas roof. Designed so that the French farmer could take a sheep to market in the back and also drive his family to the fair on Saturday, it was an unbreakable little car that suited the modest post-war requirement of the French – and many others of those austere days.

Renault matched it with the 4cv, a squat four-cylinder saloon which earned the nickname of the 'Pat of Butter' as the first models were painted in yellow ochre paint confiscated from the German Afrika Korps.

Britain offered the side-valve Minor in 1949, based on the pre-war Series E engine. Originally designed by Alec Issigonis to have torsion bar independent front suspension, front-wheel drive and a flat-four engine, it finally appeared in conventional layout, but the Minor's excellent suspension and road-holding capabilities earned it a warm welcome from drivers; today the Minor has become something of a cult automobile, mint-condition models fetching high figures.

From Ford came the Consul and the Zephyr, a four and a six respectively – two cars which made a name for Dagenham in the early

Below: Ford of Britain introduced a new Anglia and Prefect in 1953 – and for those with just £391 in the pocket, the 1172-cc Popular, hardly changed since pre-war times.

Left : The Ford Consul and Zephyr (1·5 litres, four cylinders, and 2·3 litres, six cylinders respectively) were introduced in 1951. This is one of the first Consuls, produced for six years.

Above left: Motor racing was back again by the early Fifties.

1950s. With them was a unit-constructed smaller car, the 100E Anglia, which was in fact the 1935 Popular engine with third-generation suspension and styling.

Despite its antiquity, the 100E Anglia was to become a firm favourite, not only among young families who required a cheap car, but also among rally enthusiasts, who were able to adapt the engine and beef-up the suspension.

The most technically advanced and aesthetically bold design came (as usual) from Citroën, the shape of the DS19. Looking a little shark-like, the DS – born 1955 – weighed 22 cwt, was powered by a four-cylinder 1·9-litre engine, and had powered steering, brakes and clutch, self-levelling hydropneumatic suspension, and superb streamlining – and it would motor all day long at a high, typically French, cruising speed.

A feature of the 1950s was the 'bubble-car', such as the three-wheeler Isetta Moto Coupé, the Messerschmitt, the Heinkel and the Goggomobile. An English design, the Bond Minicar was a three-wheeler with at the front the driving wheel, on which was balanced a single-cylinder two-stroke motor-cycle engine. Hard to handle and prone to lose its chain drive, the little Bond nevertheless was gratefully received by the just-under-the-four-wheel market.

A remark by Leonard Lord, boss of the new British Motor Corporation since the Morris-Austin merger killed the bubble-car market. 'Alec,' he said to designer Alec Issigonis, 'we've got to drive 'em out of the streets by designing a *proper* miniature car.' So, in the autumn of 1959 was born the Issigonis Mini, but the story of how it succeeded belongs more properly to the next ten years – the Swinging Sixties.

A unit developed from W. O. Bentley's Lagonda engine (2·6 litres, twin ohc) was put into a space frame and competed at Le Mans, becoming the Aston Martin DB2 in 1950. This DB2/4 houses an engine enlarged to 3 litres.

Overleaf: The MGA appeared (first at Le Mans) in 1955 and was unkindly compared to a 'teardrop on a movie queen's cheek' by some. The normal engine was a 1·5-litre pushrod affair, but some, such as this, sported a twin overhead camshaft engine.

Right: Rallying, racing and touring, coupled with safety and elegance – the Porsche from Stuttgart. This mud-splashed Type 356 is seen passing through an Alpine village during a Monte Carlo Rally of the late Fifties.

The Jaguar XK series would be difficult to fault aesthetically, and with its race-proved engine (five wins at Le Mans) developing 210 bhp by 1959, the XK 150 was a fitting development of the famed XK 120. It also had disc brakes all round.

Opposite page: Formula One Grand Prix Maserati 250F, 1957. Some opine that this car has the purest line of any racing car designed since pioneer days. It took J. M. Fangio to the World Championship title of 1957.

Motor sport had noisily recovered by the early 1950s and the Grand Prix Mercedes Benz took to the circuits again, pursued rather hopelessly by Ferrari, Maserati, Gordini and BRM, although by 1962 the BRM had been driven into World Championship place by Graham Hill.

At Le Mans the disaster in 1955, when Pierre Levegh's Mercedes plunged into the crowds and caused more than 80 deaths, made race organizers think seriously about audience safety. Two years later the Marquis de Portago's Ferrari killed 11 people in the Mille Miglia, resulting in the end of that spectacular road race.

The Coopers, father and son, were busy building 500-cc racing cars to fit that specialized formula; by 1957 they had developed their race-design theories into a Formula One rear-engined machine which gave Jack Brabham both the 1959 and 1960 World Championships.

Living with the Automobile

When the first of the BMC Minis appeared in 1959 under the Austin flag, it was hailed as the great breakthrough in engineering design, in fuel and space-saving, in handling, in cost – and in sheer fun-driving. All these it was and all these qualities were later copied by other manufacturers. Not that all of them considered it a practical proposition at first. . . . Ford engineers bought one and stripped it down, component by component. When they had costed its production they decided that, on the numbers which could then be sold, it would be hopelessly uneconomical for them to build anything similar. In fact, they reached the conclusion that it was probably costing BMC far more to manufacture than could ever be regained in profits – a guess which has proved accurate. But, like the internal combustion itself, the Mini survived and is still happily selling today, its transverse engine, front-wheel drive, all-independent rubber cone suspension in a body no more than 10 feet long, making it the ideal car for crowded highways of the latter half of this motoring century.

The BMC Mini heralded the 1960s. Its small dimensions, partly due to its transverse engine, made it look larger inside than out.

A 'souped-up' version, the 997-cc Mini-Cooper, appeared in 1961. Put into a miniature jeep frame, it became the Mini-Moke. In a flurry of dust and bouncing wheels, the Mini turned into the young man's rally and racing saloon. It inspired the name of the short skirt then in fashion. Its name became part of the English language.

While the years from 1960 to the present have seen many dramatic changes in motoring, it has not been a period of startling new models.

For this one must point to a number of factors – upheavals in the
Middle East, leading to vast increase in fuel prices; a rejection of the
motor-car in 'advanced' circles with a consequent demand for speed
limits which are often absurdly severe; anti-pollution lobbies
demanding impossible standards of exhaust cleanliness; and world
recession.

Perhaps the most significant advance recorded during the Sixties was
the launch of an entirely new kind of automobile power unit – the
Wankel rotary combustion engine. If theory were all, this would now be
driving every car on the road. However, the Wankel unluckily turned
up on the world's markets between 1967 and 1969, just as the design
direction headed towards fuel conservation – and the rotary was a
thirsty beast.

*Mercedes Benz
produced this
powerful C111
experimental
rotary-piston-
engined car –
then decided that
it was too
powerful for road
use.*

111

The rotary engine is one in which combustion chambers are aligned around a central pivot, from which power can be transmitted directly to the gearbox, unlike a conventional reciprocating engine in which power from the pistons must be transmitted via connecting rods to a crankshaft and flywheel to the box. By 1967 Wankel's engine had been under painful development for more than ten years, with manufacturers like General Motors and Mazda working on it under licence from the originators, NSU of Germany.

Following the rotary-engined NSU R080 came Mazda's Cosmo sports model and then the R100 in 1969. Mercedes Benz also built a dynamically beautiful sports coupé, the C111, with a four-rotor engine giving 350 bhp and a top speed of 306 km/h (190 mph). Perhaps wisely Daimler-Benz in Germany decided that this exhilarating missile was not the sort of car for the company to put into the hands of ordinary mortal motorists, and it never reached the production line.

Mazda rotary-engined Savanna RX-7. This Japanese manufacturer is now the only one to brave the market with a rotary.

After that, the Wankel went into decline. Though it was simple to maintain and almost without vibration with its low-torque fluctuations and absence of reciprocating masses, it suffered from sealing and exhaust problems . . . and when one adds the fuel factor it is not difficult to understand its almost total failure.

In Britain takeovers, amalgamations, mergers were the vogue in the Sixties, followed by rationalization (which in plain English meant that one group gobbled up another and spat out the indigestible pips). Rover took control of Alvis, then were themselves seized by Leyland two years later; the British Motor Corporation acquired Jaguar, and Leyland swallowed BMC, with results that are still producing ulcers for British Leyland today.

The Rootes Group – Hillman, Humber, Singer, *et al.* – launched the Hillman Imp, a nippy rear-engined saloon with an 875-cc engine developing 39 bhp and possessing a compression ratio of 10 : 1 and

more design faults than a clockwork television set. Production difficulties also gave the Imp a bad sales start from which it never fully
recovered, and in 1974 Chrysler took over Rootes – only to find themselves in turn being swallowed by Peugeot.

Citroën and Peugeot got their heads together in 1964 to pool ideas
for new projects, but the company did not work out. Citroën, however,
bought up the Panhard firm and then turned their attention to
Maserati, the result of which was the brilliant SM coupé, with a V6
engine and clever power steering which gave greatest assistance at low
speeds and tailed off towards the top of the range (since copied by
several other manufacturers of oriental origins).

The SM, one of the world's most advanced cars, created by brilliant
French engineers for a company that is known for its bold forward-
looking policies did nothing, sadly, to help Citroën's financial troubles.
By 1975 the French government moved in to help. Renault took over

*Germany's cross-
country vehicle,
the Mercedes-
Benz
Geländwagen,
with a choice of
diesel or petrol
engines, three
body versions and
two wheelbase
lengths.*

the company's Berliet truck business, while Peugeot – with considerable government assistance – was made responsible for cars.

Interestingly, while all this went on, Renault and Peugeot were still collaborating on engine design and building, the Renault 14 being driven by a transverse Peugeot power unit.

In Italy Lancia were also in difficulties, facing collapse by 1970 because of inability to finance a new model programme. Fiat stepped in and the new Beta range of Lancias appeared, something of a stopgap until the Gamma series was produced.

Volkswagen were drawn into the Mercedes-Auto-Union conglomerate and themselves quickly took in Audi from Daimler-Benz and bought NSU. This resulted in the VW K70, basically an NSU, which highlighted VW's move away from the rear-engined, air-cooled policy. Within a few years a striking new range of cars appeared – the Audi 50, 90 and 100, the VW Scirocco, the Golf, the Polo and the Derby.

Beetle sales, having reached the 15 million mark with ease, began to tail off and manufacture of the car was continued, from 1978, in countries like Brazil, climbing to 20 million total production.

Rover, one of the first companies to stress the constructional safety aspects of their cars, launched the 2000 in 1963. Starting as a four-cylinder of 90-plus bhp, it developed into the V8 3500 and the 2200 TC, which by 1973 was responsive to the new demands for emission control.

In 1971 Rover's famous Land-Rover, first developed in 1948 with the Rover 60 engine, was joined by the Range-Rover, powered by the Buick-originated V8 engine. Rugged and fast, with real passenger comfort which the Land-Rover usually lacked, the Range-Rover has proved a huge success.

Above: This Lincoln Continental Mark III with 7·6 litres under the 'tennis court' hood was styled a 'personal luxury car' in 1969. Ford bought the company in 1922 but has always retained the distinguished Lincoln style.

Right: Austin-Healey production began in 1953, using the Austin A90 engine and many other Austin parts, coupled with one of the most handsome sports-car bodies ever produced in Britain. By 1956 the engine was a 2 639-cc six, to be followed by a 3-litre engine in 1959. This one is a '100-Six' housing a 2 639-cc unit.

114

France's oldest existing motor manufacturer is the one-time cycle company Peugeot. This is a 504 battling through a rough patch during a Safari Rally.

First of the modern series from Volkswagen was the Golf, introduced in 1974. Over 18 million cars had left the VW factories by this date.

Scorning the idea of a new 'Mini' for the time being, Ford of Dagenham produced the Cortina in 1963, one of the most popular British cars ever made. From the first 1300-cc version, the Cortina built up a reputation as a fast, roomy saloon and went on to notch up spectacular successes in rallying, and the race-winning Lotus-Cortina, with twin ohc and an acceleration kick like a mule, was one of the most exhilarating sporting production cars of its time.

Jaguar rebuilt their sporting image with the E-type, which was first seen in a six-cylinder, 3·8-litre version in 1961. Rapidly this progressed to the 4·2-litre model, of which various versions were made up to 1971. That year saw the introduction of the 5343-cc V12 E-type and those who owned one applauded its performance – but averred that working on the engine required a team of trained monkeys in order to reach the bits and pieces! Jaguar were to follow the E-type with their XJ series, running into the 1980s, the six-cylinder cars still using the engine designed over 30 years ago.

Vauxhall, after a run of ten years with the Viva – almost every kind of model from a one litre up to a Brabham-tuned car and a powerful Viva 2300 – made their mark in the small car market in the late 1970s with the Chevette, a rugged and reliable 1256-cc hatchback which could climb to an easy 90 mph. The later Cavalier, new throughout and with advanced front-wheel drive mechanics, was introduced in 1981

The 1976 Renault 14. Product of collaboration between Renault and Peugeot, it was driven by an east-west unit made by the latter.

Overleaf: Jaguar's sporting image was enhanced by the virile E-Type of 1961, with a 3·8-litre, 265-bhp engine, independent suspension and disc brakes all round. Engine sizes quickly rose to 4·2.

117

and went straight to the top of the popularity poll for fuel-economy and handling.

The MG name, so long carried under the BL banner, disappeared as the Abingdon, England, factory closed, and for two years or so it looked as though MG had gone forever.

After their success with the Mini, BL marked time throughout the 1970s, struggling to hold on to sales and solvency, often without success. Then BL jolted the motoring world with the Mini Metro, an entirely new model set fair to rival Ford's Fiesta ... and with it, shortly after the launch, came news of an MG Metro. True, it looked just like the ordinary Metro saloon, but it had some of the MG vigour, particularly when a turbo version was developed.

Both European and American manufacturers (not only in the automotive field) suffered considerably from increasing Japanese competition during the 1970s. The Japanese invasion occurred when Europe and America were suffering from labour troubles and reduced production. With a seemingly contented labour force, and robot-operated workshops building their cars, Japan had swallowed more than 11 per cent of the new-car market in the U.S.A. by 1978.

Toyota that year produced 42·8 cars for every worker – against 14·9 at Opel, 12·5 at Renault and a mere 6·1 at Alfa Romeo. General Motors might be building five million cars in America alone, but Japan was in second place among the car-manufacturing countries. Britain's manufacturers felt the pinch in sales, and the production figure of 923,744 cars in 1980 – the lowest for 20 years – reflected the successes of the competition. Some chilly comfort might have been gained by the knowledge that France, Germany, Italy – even Sweden – saw the same decline.

In 1966 *The Wall Street Journal* had blithely forecast for the year 2000, 'a dazzling, Buck Rogers-like world of plush electronically-controlled ground vehicles and 6,000-mile-an-hour airliners.'

The first Cortina, best-selling Ford in Britain since it hit the market in 1963 (and still in top demand as a used car), was a tough conventional model with exactly the right specification for its time. In 1·2- and 1·6-litre sizes, giving 48 or 64 bhp, it was joined shortly by the more powerful GT version with 83 bhp.

Right: The 1979 family car from Chrysler U.S., the Cordoba.

Today that forecast looks doubtful. With less than two decades to go, the two certain predictions are that the internal combustion engine is likely to be with us for a long time to come very much in its present form, and that the supply of crude oil – though it may become more expensive – is going to last until well after the turn of the century, in spite of the warnings of the gloomy prophets of the mid-1970s.

The thermal and other efficiencies of engines will improve as they always have. If problems of sealing and fuel consumption are overcome, we may find that the rotary combustion engine will be used more widely than the single one now offered on the market. In some countries cars may be powered by fuels other than petrol – those developed from sugar-cane, perhaps, decomposing vegetation or other waste matter. Most of the oil companies in Europe and America already have test vehicles running on esoteric fuel mixtures such as diesel and vegetable oil.

Small car from America, the AMC Spirit Liftback. Called a 'luxury compact', this was offered in 1979 to a public that was deep in an energy crisis. Its fuel consumption was just 26·5 mpg, making it a gas-miser compared with other U.S. cars.

Right: From the U.S.A., the Jeep Chief. Its V8, 5899-cc powerpack can take it cross-country at the pace of a fast-tracked vehicle or on motorways at speeds of up to 100 mph.

What about cars powered by liquefied petroleum gas – propane, or a mix of propane and butane? There are many such vehicles on the road today, operating cleanly and well. A Ford Escort powered by LPG finished 7th in its class in the 1982 R.A.C. Rally of Great Britain. But the supply of LPG comes from the refining of crude oil into petroleum products; using it does not necessarily help conserve world resources.

Natural gas – the kind which cooks the Sunday lunch – is a strong contender in the alternative fuel stakes; it poses difficulties in storage because liquefying it calls for very high pressures, and the world's known gas reserves are being depleted rapidly.

Hydrogen as a fuel for the family car is a distinct possibility, but once again there are problems of fuel-tank storage as well as of production. The hydrogen enthusiasts usually ignore the fact that, to produce hydrogen by electrolysis of water requires plants sited in countries with natural energy in the form of hydro-electricity. At present only three per cent of the fuel requirements of the U.S.A. alone could be met by the world-wide production of hydrogen from electrolysis.

Research into an electrically-powered engine continues, as it has since the earliest days of the automobile, when the first battery-driven cars made their gentle, silent journeys from charger to charger.

Right: Porsche offered the 928 in 1978. Although not as fast as the Turbo 911, it was, inevitably, a car of speed, safety and quality. The V8, 4·5-litre unit broke with Porsche tradition – it was water-cooled and front-mounted.

Left: This Aston Martin is the four-camshaft V8 Vantage, vintage 1982 and with 5·3 litres under the bulging bonnet.

Wind-tunnel testing has enabled manufacturers to reduce drag (air resistance) in moving vehicles, cutting down fuel consumption significantly in an all-out effort to conserve dwindling supplies. This is Volkswagen's wind tunnel.

The limiting factor is still the lead-acid battery, heavy for the energy it produces, and problematic in that a single charge of the battery produces power for a comparatively short range. The re-charging of the battery is likely to consume so much fossil-fuel at the power-station end (fuelled by petroleum oil in most cases) that saving is minimal. Further-developed batteries of the sodium/sulphur or nickel/iron types may give more potent energies, but without some startling new technological development your local milkman is likely to continue his monopoly of the electric vehicle market for some time to come.

An engine patented by a Dundee clergyman, the Rev. Robert Stirling, in 1816 is another contender in the 'alternative' power plants. Like the internal combustion engine, the Stirling engine uses the expansion of a heated gas to drive a piston. The heat comes from an external source instead of from the burning of fuel inside the cylinder, and the same gas is used over and over again.

The engine needs to be built of stainless steel to withstand high temperatures, so is fairly costly to produce. For some time a 25-hp Stirling developed by a consortium of universities and manufacturers has been under test at the Royal Naval Engineering College near Plymouth. Although Stirling developments have not been in the public eye for several years, development work is still in progress, notably in the United States, and considerable advances have been made in second-generation examples of this unit.

Changes in the near future seem more likely to be attained through improvements rather than in radical innovations. New techniques in lubricating oil, for example, have resulted in light viscosity oils which improve fuel consumption by an average three per cent. New materials – aluminium alloys or plastics – for many mechanically-moving parts now decrease weight in the family car, and the use of plastics for bodywork has already brought about significant changes in body design and structure – and that use is accelerating. BL in Britain have a prototype ultra-lightweight car on the road which is reported to run at an easy 83 mpg.

With these developments will come new fundamental concepts of the automobile. Alfa Romeo are already working on a 'Bimotore' design for a V6 engine in which one bank of three cylinders would be tuned for fuel economy when idling, while the other would give high-speed performance on the open road. Drag reduction is also improving economical performance. A car's drag increases in proportion to the square of the air speed – resistance at 30 mph doubles at 42·4 mph, triples at 52 mph and quadruples at 60 mph. Wind-tunnel tests indicate clearly where designs should be aerodynamically improved to reduce drag and reduce fuel consumption.

A car from tomorrow's world is this Ford-based experimental vehicle built as part of a general study in aero-dynamics and energy-conservation.

Top: Solid-state instruments, allowing a biscuit-thin panel on the fascia – lighter, more reliable, cleaner, cheaper.

There will be many changes in the next two decades, but many familiar features will still be visible. Refinements will be marked during the next 20 years – but there will not be the dramatic developments of the science-fiction writer. Like man's recent exploration of space – we will find the truth rather more prosaic than fiction.

As you read, the motor industry is gearing up for the biggest change since Henry Ford developed the moving assembly line – production by robotics. Several have already moved into that field, notably Fiat and some of the Japanese manufacturers. Soon cars will be designed by

Above: Golf body-assembly line. Here side-panels, pan and bulkhead meet at a point where hundreds of spot-welds at a time are made without manual help.

127

Megastar II – another car of the future? This is a saloon based on the 2-litre Ford Taunus Sport. Its reduced drag lessens its thirst, its floor plan has been reduced in length, and its profile has reduced height.

computers – and once again several manufacturers have entered that arena. Controls and some operations have already become computerized on several marques, and dashboards are becoming digital. Safety factors in construction and handling are playing an immensely important role in design today. The sophisticated use of electrical power is present in a vast range of ancillary operations, from window-winding to ice-detecting.

But is there a great difference in the car from those puttering little vehicles of the dawn of motoring? The engine works on the same principles, the fuel is the same, the methods of starting, moving, stopping are very similar, the conventional layout is similar, the driver still has the same pedals and levers to manipulate as he did 80 years ago. Are we perhaps still right at the beginning of the business of personal road transport, a minute part of the way along the road of motoring history . . . ?

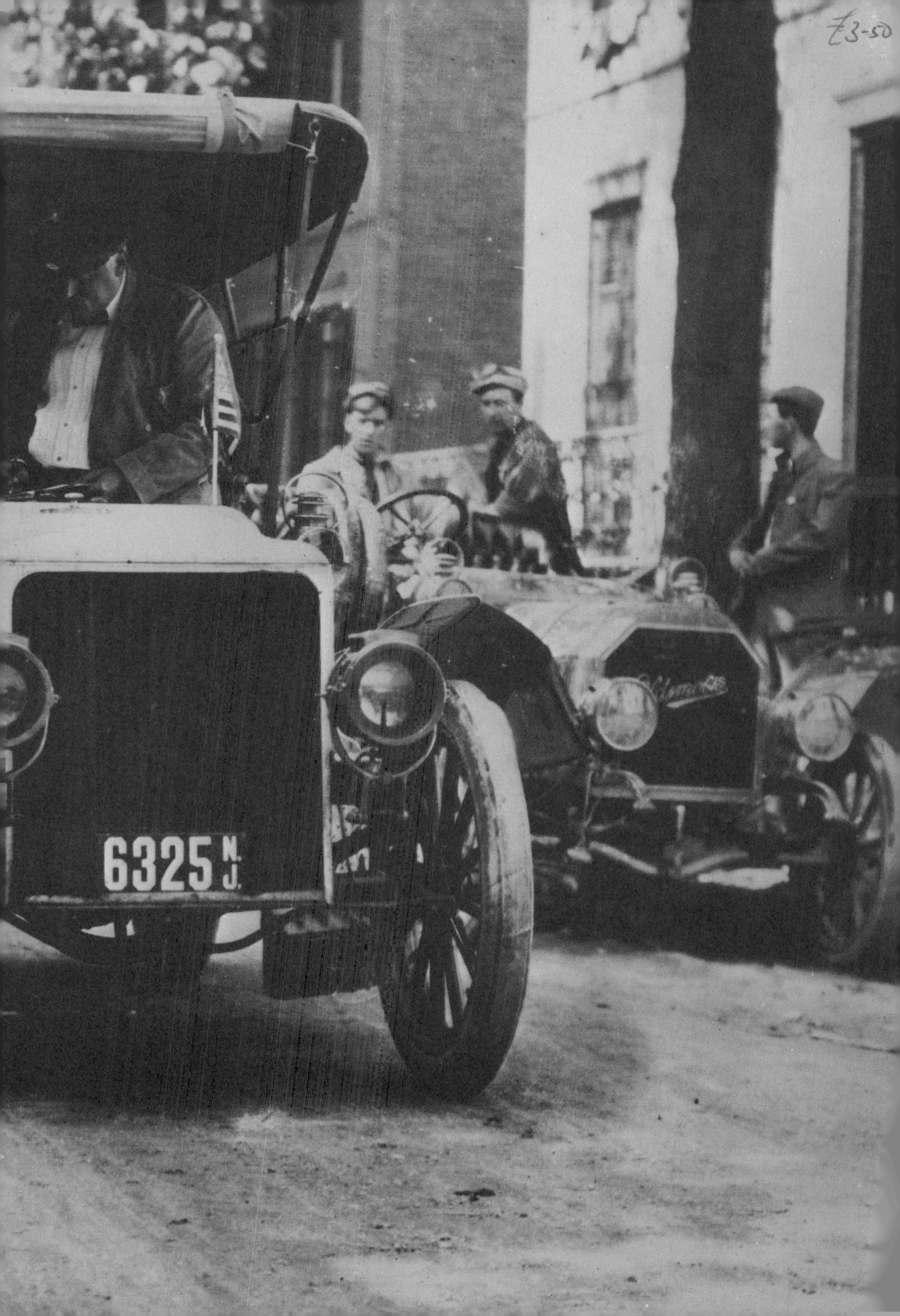
6325 N. J.

The Story of the
CAR